The Constitution

Declaration of Independence

BY

THE FOUNDING FATHERS

AND PAUL B. SKOUSEN

Foreword by

New York Times #1 Best–Selling Author Dan Clark

IZZARD INK
PUBLISHING

Izzard Ink Publishing Company
PO Box 522251
Salt Lake City, Utah 84152
www.izzardink.com

For more information about Izzard Ink Publishing or for bulk orders
please contact info@izzardink.com

Paul B. Skousen
www.paulskousen.com

Dan Clark
www.danclark.com

Designed by Alissa Rose Theodor

Softback ISBN: 978-1-63072-905-9
Hardback ISBN: 978-1-63072-906-6
eBook ISBN: 978-1-63072-907-3

"It will be of little avail to the people that the laws are made by men of their own choice if the laws be so voluminous that they cannot be read, or so incoherent that they cannot be understood."

—JAMES MADISON

Foreword

Finding Thomas Jefferson in Baghdad

In 2005, I made my first of several visits to speak to U.S. and Coalition combat troops in Southwest Asia. Over the course of sixteen days I gave 23 speeches on 12 bases and on the U.S.S. *Harry S. Truman* aircraft carrier to more than 30,000 of our bravest soldiers, airmen, sailors, and marines in Iraq, Afghanistan, Kuwait, UAE, Bahrain, and Qatar. For the first time in my life I caught a glimpse of the practical application of our United States Declaration of Independence and the deep meaning and the worldwide ramifications of our beloved Constitution.

Among the many remarkable military officers and commanders whom I met, one leader made a huge impression on me that lingers still today. His name was Colonel Blair Hansen (now Major General USAF), Commander, 332nd Air Expeditionary Wing, Balad Air Base, Iraq. After I landed in the Blackhawk and he drove me to headquarters, our conversation turned to a small book he pulled from his pocket. It was a copy of the U.S. Constitution. He carried it with him 24/7 to remind him of why he was in harm's way, away from his family, and fighting bad guys who didn't comprehend the God-given rights of every human being.

As we began our chat, Colonel Hansen made sure that I realized our American troops were not fighting for a U.S. President, or for any elected official, but only as defenders of the Constitution, and against anyone who threatens our ability to be governed by it. Within minutes, tears filled my eyes as I realized that in the military we give medals to those who willingly sacrifice themselves so that others may live; and in the corporate world we give bonuses to those who willingly sacrifice others so that they may survive. Obviously and shamefully too many have it "bass-ackwards"!

It was also in this conversation that I first learned we should never attempt to comprehend the full ramifications of our Constitution without reading the second paragraph of our incredible U.S. Declaration of Independence:

"We hold these truths to be self-evident, that all men are created equal, that they are endowed by their Creator with certain unalienable Rights, that among these are Life, Liberty and the pursuit of Happiness – that to secure these rights, Governments are instituted among Men, deriving their just powers from the consent of the governed – that whenever any Form of Government becomes destructive of these ends, it is the Right of the People to alter or to abolish it, and to institute new Government, laying its foundation on such principles and organizing its powers in such form, as to them shall seem most likely to effect their Safety and Happiness."

Our chat ended with our agreement that the Declaration of Independence was the forerunner to, and the foundation of, the U.S. Constitution, with historical documentation that Thomas Jefferson and the other Founding Fathers acknowledged their reliance on inspiration from a higher source and Supreme Being while conceiving, writing, and ratifying these two sacred documents.

The Four Principles

The Declaration's two introductory paragraphs show how it is anchored in the rock of four unalienable principles necessary for freedom anywhere in the world:

1. Rights come from God.
2. The purpose of civil government is to secure those rights.
3. The power of civil government is given by the consent of the governed, each of whom is fully entitled to rule.
4. The right to govern is forfeited by a tyrant to lower civil magistrates in order to restore the rule of law.

Divine Influence on the Constitution

Jefferson's early draft of the Declaration used the word *"derived."* Benjamin Franklin and John Adams replaced that with the phrase *"endowed by their Creator,"* which meant the Declaration rested upon rights as God had given them, not as man understood them to be. Thus, America's Founders chose to establish the new nation upon the laws of God, not upon the natural laws of man. Later, Congress inserted the adjective *certain* in the place of Jefferson's *inherent,* which Noah Webster in 1828 described to mean *"existing in something else, so as to be inseparable from it."*

The word was appropriate if man was certain about the existence of the rights being relied upon, but uncertain of their exact content. This meant that once God was identified as the giver of those rights, then the word *certain* became appropriate, because whatever God had given to mankind was, according to Noah Webster, *"sure, true, undoubted, unquestionable, existing in fact and truth"* (the definition of certain).

Obviously these and other deliberate changes in word and meaning in the Declaration had a monumental impact on the minds and hearts of every contributor to the Constitution. These words also open our minds to four facts every American should acknowledge:

Fundamental Facts

1. Historical Scholarship: Authorship of the Constitution will typically include a communal effort of Thomas Jefferson, James Madison, Thomas Paine, and John Adams. George Washington is credited with the responsibility of overseeing the Constitutional Convention that took place in Philadelphia from May 5, 1787 and September 17, 1787.

Alexander Hamilton, both a state representative from New York and a member of the Federalist Party, has been credited with the initial ideology expressed in the Constitution that stemmed from his concern over the weaknesses and inherent flaws within the Articles of Confederation, such as the requirement of 100% support on every vote for passage, and not enough power to compel the states into supporting the war. However, James Madison is generally considered to be the Father of the Constitution.

James Madison is also credited with the concept of the Bill of Rights. Based on his objection to the absence of a Constitutional Clause providing a system for both the amendment and adjustment of the original text, a clause was subsequently created rectifying these concerns. The actions of James Madison resulted in the proposal of the Bill of Rights in 1789, as well as its subsequent ratification in 1791.

2. The Duties of Freedom: *"Ask not what your country can do for you — ask what you can do for your country"* (President John F. Kennedy). **Living in America does not make you an American.** Being an American means you have read the Declaration of Independence and the Constitution so you fully understand your personal responsibility to abide by their precepts.

Being an American means you have committed yourself to some basic values and personal ethics that harmonize with eternal principles of freedom, liberty, and self-government. You are a hardworking, tax-paying, contributing citizen who has earned the right to take advantage of the prerogatives and blessings of being an American. These prerogatives are offered to those who live by the ideals, rules, and core values declared in these sacred documents — because with Rights come Responsibilities. Otherwise, we will suffer the ominous consequences referred to in the prophetic words of President Abraham Lincoln:

"From whence shall we expect the approach of danger? Shall some trans-Atlantic military giant step the earth and crush us at a blow? Never. All the armies of Europe and Asia...could not by force take a drink from the Ohio River or make a track on the Blue Ridge in the trial of a thousand years. No, if destruction be our lot we must ourselves be its author and finisher. As a nation of free men we will live forever or die by suicide."

Many people living in America take their freedom for granted. Too many of them assume the government will handle the biggest problems, and they're relieved to thank our military for serving and sacrificing and fighting because they don't have to. Therefore, we must differentiate between a "citizen mentality" and a "residence mentality" — similar to an "owner's" mentality and a "renter's" mentality. I know of no one who has ever washed and waxed and changed the oil and filter on his or her rental car before turning it back in! We take better care of that which we own — we support that which we help to create.

If we decide that this America is "our" country, and claim it in terms of "my" America, and conclude that this is where we want to live and raise our children, then don't you think we should start acting like it and be proud citizens with an "owner's men-tality" — and each do our individual part to make our country the best country in the world, full of the most significant people on the planet?

3. Because of the Brave: Our military troops are willing to fight and give their lives if necessary in order that we may remain free, leaving their families and friends to fight in faraway lands so we don't have to fight the enemy here at home. Truly, America is the land of the free *because* of the brave! May we never forget:

The Soldier

(Interchangeable with Airman, Sailor, Marine)

It is the Soldier, not the minister
Who has given us freedom of religion.

It is the Soldier, not the reporter
Who has given us freedom of the press.

It is the Soldier, not the poet
Who has given us freedom of speech.

It is the Soldier, not the campus organizer
Who has given us freedom to protest.

It is the Soldier, not the lawyer
Who has given us the right to a fair trial.

It is the Soldier, not the politician
Who has given us the right to vote.

It is the Soldier who salutes the flag,
Who serves beneath the flag,
And whose coffin is draped by the flag,
Who allows the protester to burn the flag.

© 1970 2010 Charles M. Province, U.S. Army

4. Freedom of Information: When it comes to our Constitution we must understand the phenomenon social scientists call "Confirmation Bias." Under confirmation bias, decision-makers seek out and assign more weight to evidence that confirms their hypotheses, and ignore or don't fully consider evidence negating their hypotheses. In public discussions, confirmation bias plagues us by saddling us with self-fulfilling social, political, and racial prejudices. Investigators and journalists often perpetuate confirmation bias by framing data in ways that confirm their views and personal conclusions, as in the case of the many theories on the assassination of President John F. Kennedy that to this day still stir controversy.

On a historical perspective, I believe that when the Framers of the Constitution called for the addition of a "Bill of Rights," James Madison proposed twenty constitutional amendments with the clear intent to divert confirmation bias, using strong non-debatable language that would eliminate any confusion. This was especially true in the First Amendment, which guarantees our unalienable rights to freedom of religion, speech, and the press, along with the right to protest. In his proposed draft (which was consolidated for ratification) Madison wrote:

"The civil rights of none shall be abridged on account of religious belief or worship, nor shall any national religion be established, nor shall the full and equal rights of conscience be in any manner, or on any pretext, infringed."

Two Irrefutable Examples / Collective Responsibility

Even in our 21st century that is so self-consciously politically correct, still our beloved Constitution guarantees that everybody has the privilege of worshiping or not worshiping God according to the dictates of our own conscience, with the expectation that each of us will afford one another the same privilege, especially when defending and protecting the unalienable rights of those who disagree with our theology. Those who threaten or execute "hate crimes" must be prosecuted to the full extent of the law. However, no one is a bigot because he or she disagrees with our purpose of life, our definition of marriage, or our desire to associate with our "own." The First Amendment clearly defines 'self-government' as the personal responsibility of each of us to defend the equal rights of every religion and its members to worship how, where, or what we may, protected by the rule of law.

In a different example, an equally significant Constitutional guarantee, the 15th Amendment, ratified in 1870 after the U.S. Civil War (1861-65), prohibited states from denying a male citizen the right to vote based on "race, color or previous condition of servitude." Nevertheless, in the ensuing decades, various discriminatory practices were used to prevent African Americans, particularly those in the South, from exercising their right to vote. This led my conversation with Colonel Hansen at Balad Base in Baghdad to a discussion about the historical connection that his 332nd fighter wing had with the legendary 332nd Tuskegee Red Tails.

Unlikely Role Model Heroes

Because my visit was in February, which was Black History Month, Colonel Hansen shared some incredible tales of heroism and deep dedication to duty, honor, country, and courage demonstrated by these fearless African-American fighter pilots, who in hundreds of missions, flew their P-51's as bomber escort protection and never once lost a single bomber to an enemy attack! All while they were being discriminated against back home in America: not allowed to use "white only" bathrooms, forced to enter stores, restaurants and movie theaters through the back door "black entrance," made to ride in the back of public buses, and to live their lives as second-class citizens.

"Yet," Colonel Hansen pointed out, "these brave, passionate, and proud-to-be-American 'top gun-qualified' pilots volunteered and served anyway, fueled by a belief that the promises of the Declaration and Constitution were worth fighting for, believing that one day they could enjoy their promised freedoms." Again, this illuminates the inherent and almost mystical power of the Constitution to inspire individuals to believe in life, liberty, and the pursuit of happiness.

Civil Rights

In fact, it was the Declaration and Constitution that inspired civil rights leader Dr. Martin Luther King, Jr. to boldly proclaim on August 28, 1963, in his monumental speech on the steps of the Washington D.C. Lincoln Memorial, "I have a dream that one day this nation will rise up and live out the true meaning of its creed: 'We hold these truths to be self-evident; that all men are created equal.' I have a dream that one day on the red hills of Georgia the sons of former slaves and the sons of former slave owners will be able to sit down together at the table of brotherhood. I have a dream that my four little children will one day live in a nation where they will not be judged by the color of their skin but by the content of their character."

Original Vision

The newly created United States of America first formulated her "rule of law" with the Articles of Confederation, which many historians describe as have been a reaction to the unpleasant conditions to which citizens of the United States had been subject under the rule of King George III of England. Consequently, a desperate and urgent need to replace the Articles with a better solution was rapidly gaining popularity.

Hence, the Constitution of the United States was written and ratified, and is considered to be the foremost piece of legislature. It explicitly defined the role and limitations of political power within the United States.

Unless America could adopt a central government with sufficient authority to function as a nation, the thirteen states would remain a group of insignificant, feuding little nations united by nothing more than geography, and forever vulnerable to the impositions of aggressive foreign powers. No wonder the first purpose stated in the preamble of the new United States Constitution was *"to form a more perfect union."*

Principle Centered Leadership

The success of the convention was attributable in large part to the remarkable intelligence, wisdom, and unselfishness of the delegates. As James Madison wrote in the preface to his notes on the Constitutional Convention:

"There never was an assembly of men, charged with a great and arduous trust, who were more pure in their motives, or more exclu-

sively or anxiously devoted to the object committed to them." Thus, the underlying premise of this whole constitutional order, and all the benefits and blessings enjoyed under the United States Constitution are dependent upon the rule of law and governed by the principles which it embodies. John Adams, second president of the United States, said: *"Our Constitution was made only for a moral and religious people. It is wholly inadequate to the government of any other."* Similarly, James Madison stated in his Federalist Papers that there had to be *"sufficient virtue among men for self-government because republican government presupposes the existence of these qualities in a higher degree than any other form."*

Finding Inspired Justice in the Constitution

The United States Constitution was the first written constitution of its kind in the world. It has served Americans well, enhancing freedom and prosperity during the changed conditions of more than two hundred years. Frequently copied, it has become the United States' most important export. After two centuries, every nation in the world except six have adopted written constitutions, and the U.S. Constitution was the model for nearly all of them.

Therefore, may our Supreme Court Justices, tasked with the great burden of carrying our Constitution intact and protected from one generation to the next, fully comprehend what our Founding Fathers were inspired to write. May these Justices always remember: some things are true whether you believe them or not; everybody is entitled to their own opinion, but nobody is entitled to the wrong facts; and you should never believe everything that you think.

And may our Senators, tasked with the great burden of thoroughly vetting the successors to this highest court, only consider the qualifications of the Supreme Court nominees based on the prestige of their law school, their ranking in their graduating class, the number of cases they tried and won, and their years of experience practicing law, so the confirmation process is always about choosing the best and most qualified, not about the Left and the Right

America – A Country for All Men & Women

Over the years I have returned many times to the same Middle Eastern areas to inspire and entertain our troops. My last trip was in July of 2014, when we also visited Addis Ababa and Arba Minch, Ethiopia and Djibouti, Africa. As you can imagine, each experience built on the previous one in solidifying my appreciation for our troops, the sacrifice of their families, and why and how their personal commitment to service before self is a testimony to the fact that living in America does not make you an American.

America is more than a landmass full of natural resources and beautiful, breathtaking forests, lakes, mountains, and plains. America is an experiment in self-government, founded on specific ideals and preserved through obedience to a set of morality-based core values couched in an incentive-motivated social and economic system of free enterprise. America is a land of opportunity, not entitlement, which is clearly spelled out by our inspired Founding Fathers who wrote the U.S. Constitution.

Constitutional Responsibility

As you read and re-read and study this Constitution, I trust you will conclude with a never-wavering, unshakable conviction that it is part of our civic duty to be moral in our conduct toward all people. There is no place in responsible citizenship for dishonesty or deceit or for willful law-breaking of any kind. As a group of immigrants from every race, color, and creed, who have all arrived in America on different ships originally, but are all in the same boat now, may we unite as citizens living together as "one nation, under God, indivisible, with liberty and justice for all."

In the words of one of our greatest Americans, President Ronald Reagan, *"America was founded on a dream, and now it's your turn to keep that dream moving. We've always reached for a new spirit and aimed at a higher goal. We've always been courageous, determined, unafraid, and bold. Who among us ever wants to say we no longer have those qualities? We look to you to meet the great challenge, to reach beyond the commonplace and not fall short for lack of creativity and courage. And to do this? All you need to begin with is a dream to do better than ever before. All you need is to have faith and that dream will come true. All you need to do is act, and the time for action is now!"*

God bless America and everyone who lives in accordance with the principles and precepts illuminated in our divinely inspired Declaration of Independence, held accountable by our beloved and sacred Constitution!

Dan Clark
National Speaker Hall of Fame &
author of "The Art of Significance"
July 4, 2016
www.danclark.com

Preface

America's two founding documents are not difficult to read if you start with a basic knowledge of their structure and content. With a few simple pointers you will discover these documents have more answers to today's perplexing challenges than people realize.

As a starting place, learn these basic ideas:

The Number 27
You can remember some general ideas about these documents using the number 27.
There are 27 rights protected in the Bill of Rights.
There are 27 charges made against King George III in the Declaration.
There are 27 Amendments to the Constitution.

The Declaration has five parts
1) **Preamble:** This short statement introduces the subject with these famous word, "When in the course of human events...."
2) **Assertions:** This describes the eight ancient principles of freedom and unalienable human rights. It starts with these famous words, "We hold these truths to be self-evident...."
3) **The Charges:** This section lists 27 acts of tyranny and despotism committed by King George III against the colonists over a 15 years period.

4) **The Defense:** These two paragraphs list those actions the colonists took to peacefully resolve their differences with the King.

5) **The Declaration:** The last paragraph is the actual declaration of independence from both the King and from his parliament.

It will take you about 10 minutes to read the Declaration.

The Constitution has seven basic parts called Articles

1) Article I is the job description of Congress. It is the Legislative Branch.

2) Article II is the job description of the president. It is the Executive Branch.

3) Article III is the job description of the Supreme Court. It is the Judiciary Branch.

4) Article IV describes the role of the states and their relationship with the federal government.

5) Article V describes how to amend the Constitution

6) Article VI declares the Constitution as the supreme law of the land and puts elected officers under oath to uphold and defend it.

7) Article VII explains how the Constitution was to be ratified.

It will take you about 30 minutes to read the seven Articles, and another 10 minutes to read the Bill of Rights.

Ten Common Myths

A lot of bad information about the Constitution is becoming accepted as fact. Learn the truth in the section, "Ten Common Myths About the Constitution."

Finally, a Good Glossary of Terms

Most people lose interest in these documents because the vocabulary is a little different. Check the glossary for fast help on words that don't make sense.

It's a Preview

This introduction to the Declaration and the Constitution is a preview of a published primer on the Constitution entitled "How to Read the Constitution and the Declaration of Independence," by Paul B. Skousen and published by Izzard Ink. It is available at bookstores everywhere.

Make it a Habit

Make it a habit, an annual immersion into the politics of freedom, to read these two documents regularly.

July 4th is a perfect time to read the Declaration of Independence, and be reminded of the foundation ideas that created the greatest freedom formula in the history of the world.

September 17th is the birthday of the Constitution. That's an ideal day to read the seven articles as a refresher on the limitations and constraints we put on the political leaders who lead and guide the United States of America.

These documents can be the most satisfying reading by every freedom-loving individual around the world, and they will not disappoint.

Contents

The Declaration of Independence

IN CONGRESS, July 4, 1776.

The unanimous Declaration
of the thirteen
United States of America

When in the Course of human events, it becomes necessary for one people to dissolve the political bands which have connected them with another, and to assume among the powers of the earth, the separate and equal station to which the Laws of Nature and of Nature's God entitle them, a decent respect to the opinions of mankind requires that they should declare the causes which impel them to the separation.

We hold these truths to be self-evident, that all men are created equal, that they are endowed by their Creator with certain unalienable Rights, that among these are Life, Liberty and the pursuit of Happiness.—That to secure these rights, Governments are instituted among Men, deriving their just powers from the consent of the governed, —That whenever any Form of Government becomes destructive of these ends, it is the Right of the People to alter or to abolish it, and to institute new Government, laying its foundation on such principles and organizing its powers in such form, as to them shall seem most likely to effect their Safety and Happiness. Prudence, indeed, will dictate that Governments long established should not be changed for light and transient causes; and accordingly all experience hath shewn, that mankind are more disposed to suffer, while evils are sufferable, than to right themselves by abolishing the forms to which they are accustomed. But when a long train of abuses and usurpations, pursuing invariably the same Object evinces a design to reduce them under absolute Despotism, it is their right, it is their duty, to throw off such Government, and to provide new Guards for their future security.—Such has been the patient sufferance of these Colonies; and such is now the necessity which constrains them to alter their former Systems of Government. The history of the present King of Great Britain is a history of repeated injuries and usurpations, all having in direct object the establishment of an absolute Tyranny over these States. To prove this, let Facts be submitted to a candid world.

He has refused his Assent to Laws, the most wholesome and necessary for the public good.

He has forbidden his Governors to pass Laws of immediate and pressing importance, unless suspended in their operation till his Assent should be obtained; and when so suspended, he has utterly neglected to attend to them.

He has refused to pass other Laws for the accommodation of large districts of people, unless those people would relinquish the right of Representation in the Legislature, a right inestimable to them and formidable to tyrants only.

He has called together legislative bodies at places unusual, uncomfortable, and distant from the depository of their public Records, for the sole purpose of fatiguing them into compliance with his measures.

He has dissolved Representative Houses repeatedly, for opposing with manly firmness his invasions on the rights of the people.

He has refused for a long time, after such dissolutions, to cause others to be elected; whereby the Legislative powers, incapable of Annihilation, have returned to the People at large for their exercise; the State remaining in the mean time exposed to all the dangers of invasion from without, and convulsions within.

HE has endeavoured to prevent the population of these States; for that purpose obstructing the Laws for Naturalization of Foreigners; refusing to pass others to encourage their migrations hither, and raising the conditions of new Appropriations of Lands.

HE has obstructed the Administration of Justice, by refusing his Assent to Laws for establishing Judiciary powers.

HE has made Judges dependent on his Will alone, for the tenure of their offices, and the amount and payment of their salaries.

HE has erected a multitude of New Offices, and sent hither swarms of Officers to harass our people, and eat out their substance.

HE has kept among us, in times of peace, Standing Armies without the Consent of our legislatures.

HE has affected to render the Military independent of and superior to the Civil power.

HE has combined with others to subject us to a jurisdiction foreign to our constitution, and unacknowledged by our laws; giving his Assent to their Acts of pretended Legislation:

FOR Quartering large bodies of armed troops among us:

FOR protecting them, by a mock Trial, from punishment for any Murders which they should commit on the Inhabitants of these States:

FOR cutting off our Trade with all parts of the world:

FOR imposing Taxes on us without our Consent:

FOR depriving us in many cases, of the benefits of Trial by Jury:

FOR transporting us beyond Seas to be tried for pretended offences:

FOR abolishing the free System of English Laws in a

neighboring Province, establishing therein an Arbitrary government, and enlarging its Boundaries so as to render it at once an example and fit instrument for introducing the same absolute rule into these Colonies:

FOR taking away our Charters, abolishing our most valuable Laws, and altering fundamentally the Forms of our Governments:

FOR suspending our own Legislatures, and declaring themselves invested with power to legislate for us in all cases whatsoever.

HE has abdicated Government here, by declaring us out of his Protection and waging War against us.

HE has plundered our seas, ravaged our Coasts, burnt our towns, and destroyed the lives of our people.

HE is at this time transporting large Armies of foreign Mercenaries to compleat the works of death, desolation and tyranny, already begun with circumstances of Cruelty & perfidy scarcely paralleled in the most barbarous ages, and totally unworthy the Head of a civilized nation.

HE has constrained our fellow Citizens taken Captive on the high Seas to bear Arms against their Country, to become the executioners of their friends and Brethren, or to fall themselves by their Hands.

HE has excited domestic insurrections amongst us, and has endeavoured to bring on the inhabitants of our frontiers, the merciless Indian Savages, whose known rule of warfare, is an undistinguished destruction of all ages, sexes and conditions.

IN every stage of these Oppressions We have Petitioned for Redress in the most humble terms: Our repeated Petitions have been answered only by repeated injury. A Prince whose character is thus marked by every act which may define a Tyrant, is unfit to be the ruler of a free people.

NOR have We been wanting in attentions to our British brethren. We have warned them from time to time of attempts by

6

their legislature to extend an unwarrantable jurisdiction over us. We have reminded them of the circumstances of our emigration and settlement here. We have appealed to their native justice and magnanimity, and we have conjured them by the ties of our common kindred to disavow these usurpations, which, would inevitably interrupt our connections and correspondence. They too have been deaf to the voice of justice and of consanguinity. We must, therefore, acquiesce in the necessity, which denounces our Separation, and hold them, as we hold the rest of mankind, Enemies in War, in Peace Friends.

WE, therefore, the Representatives of the UNITED STATES OF AMERICA, in General Congress, Assembled, appealing to the Supreme Judge of the world for the rectitude of our intentions, do, in the Name, and by Authority of the good People of these Colonies, solemnly publish and declare, That these United Colonies are, and of Right ought to be Free and Independent States; that they are Absolved from all Allegiance to the British Crown, and that all political connection between them and the State of Great Britain, is and ought to be totally dissolved; and that as Free and Independent States, they have full Power to levy War, conclude Peace, contract Alliances, establish Commerce, and to do all other Acts and Things which Independent States may of right do. And for the support of this Declaration, with a firm reliance on the protection of divine Providence, we mutually pledge to each other our Lives, our Fortunes and our sacred Honor.

The 56 signatures on the Declaration of Independence
(In the order that they appear on the document)

Georgia:
>Button Gwinnett
>Lyman Hall
>George Walton

North Carolina:
>William Hooper
>Joseph Hewes
>John Penn

South Carolina:
>Edward Rutledge
>Thomas Heyward, Jr.
>Thomas Lynch, Jr.
>Arthur Middleton

Massachusetts:
>John Hancock

Maryland:
>Samuel Chase
>William Paca
>Thomas Stone
>Charles Carroll of
>Carrollton

Virginia:
>George Wythe
>Richard Henry Lee
>Thomas Jefferson
>Benjamin Harrison
>Thomas Nelson, Jr.

Francis Lightfoot Lee
Carter Braxton

Pennsylvania:
>Robert Morris
>Benjamin Rush
>Benjamin Franklin
>John Morton
>George Clymer
>James Smith
>George Taylor
>James Wilson
>George Ross

Delaware:
>Caesar Rodney
>George Read
>Thomas McKean

New York:
>William Floyd
>Philip Livingston
>Francis Lewis
>Lewis Morris

New Jersey:
>Richard Stockton
>John Witherspoon
>Francis Hopkinson
>John Hart
>Abraham Clark

New Hampshire:

> Josiah Bartlett
>
> William Whipple

Massachusetts:

> Samuel Adams
>
> John Adams
>
> Robert Treat Paine
>
> Elbridge Gerry

Rhode Island:

> Stephen Hopkins
>
> William Ellery

Connecticut:

> Roger Sherman
>
> Samuel Huntington
>
> William Williams
>
> Oliver Wolcott

New Hampshire:

> Matthew Thornton

CONSTITUTION OF
THE UNITED STATES

We the People of the United States, in Order to form a more perfect Union, establish Justice, insure domestic Tranquility, provide for the common defence, promote the general Welfare, and secure the Blessings of Liberty to ourselves and our Posterity, do ordain and establish this Constitution for the United States of America.

Article I.

SECTION 1. All legislative Powers herein granted shall be vested in a Congress of the United States, which shall consist of a Senate and House of Representatives.

SECTION 2. The House of Representatives shall be composed of Members chosen every second Year by the People of the several States, and the Electors in each State shall have the Qualifications requisite for Electors of the most numerous Branch of the State Legislature.

No Person shall be a Representative who shall not have attained to the Age of twenty five Years, and been seven Years a Citizen of the United States, and who shall not, when elected, be an Inhabitant of that State in which he shall be chosen.

[Representatives and direct Taxes shall be apportioned among the several States which may be included within this Union, according to their respective Numbers, which shall be determined by adding to the whole Number of free Persons, including those bound to Service for a Term of Years, and excluding Indians not taxed, three fifths of all other Persons.][1] The actual Enumeration shall be made within three Years after the first Meeting of the Congress of the United States, and within every subsequent Term of ten Years, in such Manner as they shall by Law direct. The Number of Representatives shall not exceed one for every thirty Thousand, but each State shall have at Least one Representative; and until such enumeration shall be made, the State of New Hampshire shall be entitled to choose three, Massachusetts eight, Rhode Island and Providence Plantations one, Connecticut five, New York six, New Jersey four, Pennsylvania eight, Delaware one, Maryland six, Virginia ten, North Carolina five, South Carolina five and Georgia three.

When vacancies happen in the Representation from any State, the Executive Authority thereof shall issue Writs of Election to fill such Vacancies.

The House of Representatives shall choose their Speaker and other Officers; and shall have the sole Power of Impeachment.

SECTION 3. The Senate of the United States shall be composed of two Senators from each State, [chosen by the Legislature thereof,][2] for six Years; and each Senator shall have one Vote.

Immediately after they shall be assembled in Consequence of the first Election, they shall be divided as equally as may be into three Classes. The Seats of the Senators of the first Class shall be vacated at the Expiration of the second Year, of the second Class at the Expiration of the fourth Year, and of the third Class at the Expiration of the sixth Year, so that one third may be chosen every second Year; [and if Vacancies happen by Resignation, or otherwise, during the Recess of the Legislature of any State,

---

1 Changed by section 2 of the Fourteenth Amendment.

2 Changed by the Seventeenth Amendment.

the Executive thereof may make temporary Appointments until the next Meeting of the Legislature, which shall then fill such Vacancies.][3]

No person shall be a Senator who shall not have attained to the Age of thirty Years, and been nine Years a Citizen of the United States, and who shall not, when elected, be an Inhabitant of that State for which he shall be chosen.

The Vice President of the United States shall be President of the Senate, but shall have no Vote, unless they be equally divided.

The Senate shall choose their other Officers, and also a President pro tempore, in the absence of the Vice President, or when he shall exercise the Office of President of the United States.

The Senate shall have the sole Power to try all Impeachments. When sitting for that Purpose, they shall be on Oath or Affirmation. When the President of the United States is tried, the Chief Justice shall preside: And no Person shall be convicted without the Concurrence of two thirds of the Members present.

Judgment in Cases of Impeachment shall not extend further than to removal from Office, and disqualification to hold and enjoy any Office of honor, Trust or Profit under the United States: but the Party convicted shall nevertheless be liable and subject to Indictment, Trial, Judgment and Punishment, according to Law.

SECTION 4. The Times, Places and Manner of holding Elections for Senators and Representatives, shall be prescribed in each State by the Legislature thereof; but the Congress may at any time by Law make or alter such Regulations, except as to the Place of Choosing Senators.

The Congress shall assemble at least once in every

---

3 Changed by the Seventeenth Amendment.

Year, and such Meeting shall be [on the first Monday in December,][4] unless they shall by Law appoint a different Day.

SECTION 5. Each House shall be the Judge of the Elections, Returns and Qualifications of its own Members, and a Majority of each shall constitute a Quorum to do Business; but a smaller number may adjourn from day to day, and may be authorized to compel the Attendance of absent Members, in such Manner, and under such Penalties as each House may provide.

Each House may determine the Rules of its Proceedings, punish its Members for disorderly Behavior, and, with the Concurrence of two-thirds, expel a Member.

Each House shall keep a Journal of its Proceedings, and from time to time publish the same, excepting such Parts as may in their Judgment require Secrecy; and the Yeas and Nays of the Members of either House on any question shall, at the Desire of one fifth of those Present, be entered on the Journal.

Neither House, during the Session of Congress, shall, without the Consent of the other, adjourn for more than three days, nor to any other Place than that in which the two Houses shall be sitting.

SECTION 6. The Senators and Representatives shall receive a Compensation for their Services, to be ascertained by Law, and paid out of the Treasury of the United States. They shall in all Cases, except Treason, Felony and Breach of the Peace, be privileged from Arrest during their Attendance at the Session of their respective Houses, and in going to and returning from the same; and for any Speech or Debate in either House, they shall not be questioned in any other Place.

---

4 Changed by Section 2 of the Twentieth Amendment.

No Senator or Representative shall, during the Time for which he was elected, be appointed to any civil Office under the Authority of the United States which shall have been created, or the Emoluments whereof shall have been increased during such time; and no Person holding any Office under the United States, shall be a Member of either House during his Continuance in Office.

SECTION 7. All bills for raising Revenue shall originate in the House of Representatives; but the Senate may propose or concur with Amendments as on other Bills.

Every Bill which shall have passed the House of Representatives and the Senate, shall, before it become a Law, be presented to the President of the United States; If he approve he shall sign it, but if not he shall return it, with his Objections to that House in which it shall have originated, who shall enter the Objections at large on their Journal, and proceed to reconsider it. If after such Reconsideration two thirds of that House shall agree to pass the Bill, it shall be sent, together with the Objections, to the other House, by which it shall likewise be reconsidered, and if approved by two thirds of that House, it shall become a Law. But in all such Cases the Votes of both Houses shall be determined by Yeas and Nays, and the Names of the Persons voting for and against the Bill shall be entered on the Journal of each House respectively. If any Bill shall not be returned by the President within ten Days (Sundays excepted) after it shall have been presented to him, the Same shall be a Law, in like Manner as if he had signed it, unless the Congress by their Adjournment prevent its Return, in which Case it shall not be a Law.

Every Order, Resolution, or Vote to which the Concurrence of the Senate and House of Representatives may be necessary (except on a question of Adjournment) shall be presented to the President of the United States;

and before the Same shall take Effect, shall be approved by him, or being disapproved by him, shall be repassed by two thirds of the Senate and House of Representatives, according to the Rules and Limitations prescribed in the Case of a Bill.

SECTION 8. The Congress shall have Power To lay and collect Taxes, Duties, Imposts and Excises, to pay the Debts and provide for the common Defence and general Welfare of the United States; but all Duties, Imposts and Excises shall be uniform throughout the United States;

To borrow money on the credit of the United States;

To regulate Commerce with foreign Nations, and among the several States, and with the Indian Tribes;

To establish an uniform Rule of Naturalization, and uniform Laws on the subject of Bankruptcies throughout the United States;

To coin Money, regulate the Value thereof, and of foreign Coin, and fix the Standard of Weights and Measures;

To provide for the Punishment of counterfeiting the Securities and current Coin of the United States;

To establish Post Offices and Post Roads;

To promote the Progress of Science and useful Arts, by securing for limited Times to Authors and Inventors the exclusive Right to their respective Writings and Discoveries;

To constitute Tribunals inferior to the supreme Court;

To define and punish Piracies and Felonies committed on the high Seas, and Offenses against the Law of Nations;

To declare War, grant Letters of Marque and Reprisal, and make Rules concerning Captures on Land and Water;

To raise and support Armies, but no Appropriation of Money to that Use shall be for a longer Term than two Years;

To provide and maintain a Navy;

To make Rules for the Government and Regulation of the land and naval Forces;

To provide for calling forth the Militia to execute the Laws of the Union, suppress Insurrections and repel Invasions;

To provide for organizing, arming, and disciplining, the Militia, and for governing such Part of them as may be employed in the Service of the United States, reserving to the States respectively, the Appointment of the Officers, and the Authority of training the Militia according to the discipline prescribed by Congress;

To exercise exclusive Legislation in all Cases whatsoever, over such District (not exceeding ten Miles square) as may, by Cession of particular States, and the acceptance of Congress, become the Seat of the Government of the United States, and to exercise like Authority over all Places purchased by the Consent of the Legislature of the State in which the Same shall be, for the Erection of Forts, Magazines, Arsenals, dock-Yards, and other needful Buildings; And To make all Laws which shall be necessary and proper for carrying into Execution the foregoing Powers, and all other Powers vested by this Constitution in the Government of the United States, or in any Department or Officer thereof.

SECTION 9. The Migration or Importation of such Persons as any of the States now existing shall think proper to admit, shall not be prohibited by the Congress prior to the Year one thousand eight hundred and eight, but a tax or duty may be imposed on such Importation, not exceeding ten dollars for each Person.

The privilege of the Writ of Habeas Corpus shall not be suspended, unless when in Cases of Rebellion or Invasion the public Safety may require it.

No Bill of Attainder or ex post facto Law shall be passed.

No capitation, or other direct, Tax shall be laid, unless in Proportion to the Census or Enumeration here in before directed to be taken.[5]

No Tax or Duty shall be laid on Articles exported from any State.

No Preference shall be given by any Regulation of Commerce or Revenue to the Ports of one State over those of another: nor shall Vessels bound to, or from, one State, be obliged to enter, clear, or pay Duties in another.

No Money shall be drawn from the Treasury, but in Consequence of Appropriations made by Law; and a regular Statement and Account of the Receipts and Expenditures of all public Money shall be published from time to time.

No Title of Nobility shall be granted by the United States: And no Person holding any Office of Profit or Trust under them, shall, without the Consent of the Congress, accept of any present, Emolument, Office, or Title, of any kind whatever, from any King, Prince or foreign State.

SECTION 10. No State shall enter into any Treaty, Alliance, or Confederation; grant Letters of Marque and Reprisal; coin Money; emit Bills of Credit; make any Thing but gold and silver Coin a Tender in Payment of Debts; pass any Bill of Attainder, ex post facto Law, or Law impairing the Obligation of Contracts, or grant any Title of Nobility.

No State shall, without the Consent of the Congress, lay any Imposts or Duties on Imports or Exports, except what may be absolutely necessary for executing its inspection Laws: and the net Produce of all Duties and Imposts, laid by any State on Imports or Exports, shall be for the Use of the Treasury of the United States; and all such Laws shall be subject to the Revision and Control of the Congress.

No State shall, without the Consent of Congress,

---

5 Changed by the Sixteenth Amendment.

lay any duty of Tonnage, keep Troops, or Ships of War in time of Peace, enter into any Agreement or Compact with another State, or with a foreign Power, or engage in War, unless actually invaded, or in such imminent Danger as will not admit of delay.

Article II.

SECTION 1. The executive Power shall be vested in a President of the United States of America. He shall hold his Office during the Term of four Years, and, together with the Vice-President chosen for the same Term, be elected, as follows:

Each State shall appoint, in such Manner as the Legislature thereof may direct, a Number of Electors, equal to the whole Number of Senators and Representatives to which the State may be entitled in the Congress: but no Senator or Representative, or Person holding an Office of Trust or Profit under the United States, shall be appointed an Elector.

[The Electors shall meet in their respective States, and vote by Ballot for two persons, of whom one at least shall not lie an Inhabitant of the same State with themselves. And they shall make a List of all the Persons voted for, and of the Number of Votes for each; which List they shall sign and certify, and transmit sealed to the Seat of the Government of the United States, directed to the President of the Senate. The President of the Senate shall, in the Presence of the Senate and House of Representatives, open all the Certificates, and the Votes shall then be counted. The Person having the greatest Number of Votes shall be the President, if such Number be a Majority of the whole Number of Electors appointed; and if there be more than one who have such Majority, and have an equal Number of Votes, then the House of Representatives shall immediately choose by Ballot one of them for President; and if no Person have a Majority, then from the five highest on the List the said House shall in like Manner choose the President. But in choosing the President, the Votes shall be taken by States, the Representation from each State having one Vote; a quorum for this Purpose shall consist of a Member or Members from two-thirds of the States, and a Majority of all the States shall be necessary to a Choice. In every Case, after the Choice of the President, the Person having the greatest Number of Votes of the Electors shall be the Vice President. But if there should remain two or more who have equal Votes, the Senate shall choose from them by Ballot the Vice-President.][6]

The Congress may determine the Time of choosing the Electors, and the Day on which they shall give their Votes; which Day shall be the same throughout the United States.

No person except a natural born Citizen, or a Citizen of the United States, at the time of the Adoption of this Constitution, shall be eligible to the Office of President; neither shall any Person be eligible to that Office who shall not have attained to the Age of thirty-five Years, and been fourteen Years a Resident within the United States.

[In Case of the Removal of the President from Office, or of his Death, Resignation, or Inability to discharge the Powers and Duties of the said Office, the same shall devolve on the Vice President, and the Congress may by Law provide for the Case of Removal, Death, Resignation or Inability, both of the President and Vice President, declaring what Officer shall then act as President, and such Officer shall act accordingly, until the Disability be removed, or a President shall be elected.][7]

---

6 Changed by the Twelfth Amendment.
7 Changed by the Twenty-Fifth Amendment.

The President shall, at stated Times, receive for his Services, a Compensation, which shall neither be increased nor diminished during the Period for which he shall have been elected, and he shall not receive within that Period any other Emolument from the United States, or any of them.

Before he enter on the Execution of his Office, he shall take the following Oath or Affirmation:

"I do solemnly swear (or affirm) that I will faithfully execute the Office of President of the United States, and will to the best of my Ability, preserve, protect and defend the Constitution of the United States."

SECTION 2. The President shall be Commander in Chief of the Army and Navy of the United States, and of the Militia of the several States, when called into the actual Service of the United States; he may require the Opinion, in writing, of the principal Officer in each of the executive Departments, upon any subject relating to the Duties of their respective Offices, and he shall have Power to Grant Reprieves and Pardons for Offenses against the United States, except in Cases of Impeachment.

He shall have Power, by and with the Advice and Consent of the Senate, to make Treaties, provided two thirds of the Senators present concur; and he shall nominate, and by and with the Advice and Consent of the Senate, shall appoint Ambassadors, other public Ministers and Consuls, Judges of the supreme Court, and all other Officers of the United States, whose Appointments are not herein otherwise provided for, and which shall be established by Law: but the Congress may by Law vest the Appointment of such inferior Officers, as they think proper, in the President alone, in the Courts of Law, or in the Heads of Departments.

The President shall have Power to fill up all Vacancies

that may happen during the Recess of the Senate, by granting Commissions which shall expire at the End of their next Session.

SECTION 3. He shall from time to time give to the Congress Information of the State of the Union, and recommend to their Consideration such Measures as he shall judge necessary and expedient; he may, on extraordinary Occasions, convene both Houses, or either of them, and in Case of Disagreement between them, with Respect to the Time of Adjournment, he may adjourn them to such Time as he shall think proper; he shall receive Ambassadors and other public Ministers; he shall take Care that the Laws be faithfully executed, and shall Commission all the Officers of the United States.

SECTION 4. The President, Vice President and all civil Officers of the United States, shall be removed from Office on Impeachment for, and Conviction of, Treason, Bribery, or other high Crimes and Misdemeanors.

Article III.

SECTION 1. The judicial Power of the United States, shall be vested in one supreme Court, and in such inferior Courts as the Congress may from time to time ordain and establish. The Judges, both of the supreme and inferior Courts, shall hold their Offices during good Behavior, and shall, at stated Times, receive for their Services a Compensation which shall not be diminished during their Continuance in Office.

SECTION 2. The judicial Power shall extend to all Cases, in Law and Equity, arising under this Constitution, the Laws of the United States, and Treaties made, or which shall be made, under their Authority; to all Cases affecting Ambassadors, other public Ministers and Consuls; to all Cases of admiralty and maritime Jurisdiction; to Controversies to which the United States shall be a Party; to Controversies between two or more States; [between a State and Citizens of another State;][8] between Citizens of different States; between Citizens of the same State claiming Lands under Grants of different States, [and between a State, orthe Citizens thereof, and foreign States, Citizens or Subjects.][9]

In all Cases affecting Ambassadors, other public Ministers and Consuls, and those in which a State shall be Party, the supreme Court shall have original Jurisdiction. In all the other Cases before mentioned, the supreme Court shall have appellate Jurisdiction, both as to Law and Fact, with such Exceptions, and under such Regulations as the Congress shall make.

The Trial of all Crimes, except in Cases of Impeachment, shall be by Jury; and such Trial shall be held in the State where the said Crimes shall have been committed; but when not committed within any State, the Trial shall be at such Place or Places as the Congress may by Law have directed.

SECTION 3. Treason against the United States, shall consist only in levying War against them, or in adhering to their Enemies, giving them Aid and Comfort. No Person shall be convicted of Treason unless on the Testimony of two Witnesses to the same overt Act, or on Confession in open Court.

The Congress shall have power to declare the Punishment of Treason, but no Attainder of Treason shall work Corruption of Blood, or Forfeiture except during the Life of the Person attainted.

---

8 Changed by the Eleventh Amendment.

9 Changed by the Eleventh Amendment.

Article IV.

SECTION 1. Full Faith and Credit shall be given in each State to the public Acts, Records, and judicial Proceedings of every other State. And the Congress may by general Laws prescribe the Manner in which such Acts, Records and Proceedings shall be proved, and the Effect thereof.

SECTION 2. The Citizens of each State shall be entitled to all Privileges and Immunities of Citizens in the several States.

A Person charged in any State with Treason, Felony, or other Crime, who shall flee from Justice, and be found in another State, shall on demand of the executive Authority of the State from which he fled, be delivered up, to be removed to the State having Jurisdiction of the Crime.

[No Person held to Service or Labour in one State, under the Laws thereof, escaping into another, shall, in Consequence of any Law or Regulation therein, be discharged from such Service or Labour, But shall be delivered up on Claim of the Party to whom such Service or Labour may be due.][10]

SECTION 3. New States may be admitted by the Congress into this Union; but no new States shall be formed or erected within the Jurisdiction of any other State; nor any State be formed by the Junction of two or more States, or parts of States,without the Consent of the Legislatures of the States concerned as well as of the Congress.

The Congress shall have Power to dispose of and make all needful Rules and Regulations respecting the Territory or other Property belonging to the United States; and nothing in this Constitution shall be so construed as to Prejudice any Claims of the United States, or of any particular State.

---

10 Changed by the Thirteenth Amendment.

SECTION 4. The United States shall guarantee to every State in this Union a Republican Form of Government, and shall protect each of them against Invasion; and on Application of the Legislature, or of the Executive (when the Legislature cannot be convened) against domestic Violence.

Article V.

The Congress, whenever two thirds of both Houses shall deem it necessary, shall propose Amendments to this Constitution, or, on the Application of the Legislatures of two thirds of the several States, shall call a Convention for proposing Amendments, which, in either Case, shall be valid to all Intents and Purposes, as part of this Constitution, when ratified by the Legislatures of three fourths of the several States, or by Conventions in three fourths thereof, as the one or the other Mode of Ratification may be proposed by the Congress; Provided that no Amendment which may be made prior to the Year One thousand eight hundred and eight shall in any Manner affect the first and fourth Clauses in the Ninth Section of the first Article; and that no State, without its Consent, shall be deprived of its equal Suffrage in the Senate.

Article VI.

All Debts contracted and Engagements entered into, before the Adoption of this Constitution, shall be as valid against the United States under this Constitution, as under the Confederation.

This Constitution, and the Laws of the United States which shall be made in Pursuance thereof; and all Treaties made, or which shall be made, under the Authority of the United States, shall be the supreme Law of the Land; and the Judges in every State shall be bound thereby, any Thing in the Constitution or Laws of any State to the Contrary notwithstanding.

The Senators and Representatives before mentioned, and the Members of the several State Legislatures, and all executive and judicial Officers, both of the United States and of the several States, shall be bound by Oath or Affirmation, to support this Constitution; but no religious Test shall ever be required as a Qualification to any Office or public Trust under the United States.

Article VII.

The Ratification of the Conventions of nine States, shall be sufficient for the Establishment of this Constitution between the States so ratifying the Same.

Done in Convention by the Unanimous Consent of the States present the Seventeenth Day of September in the Year of our Lord one thousand seven hundred and Eighty seven and of the Independence of the United States of America the Twelfth. In Witness whereof We have hereunto subscribed our Names.

G. Washington —
President and deputy from Virginia

New Hampshire	John Langdon Nicholas Gilman
Massachusetts	Nathaniel Gorham Rufus King
Connecticut	William Samuel Johnson Roger Sherman
New York	Alexander Hamilton
New Jersey	William Livingston David Brearley William Paterson Jonathan Dayton
Pennsylvania	Benjamin Franklin Thomas Mifflin Robert Morris George Clymer Thomas Fitzsimons Jared Ingersoll James Wilson Gouvernour Morris
Delaware	George Read Gunning Bedford Jr. John Dickinson Richard Bassett Jacob Broom
Maryland	James McHenry Daniel of St Thomas Jenifer Daniel Carroll
Virginia	John Blair James Madison Jr.
North Carolina	William Blount, Richard Dobbs Spaight Hugh Williamson
South Carolina	John Rutledge Charles Cotesworth Pinckney Charles Pinckney Pierce Butler
Georgia	William Few Abraham Baldwin Attest: William Jackson, Secretary

Amendments to the Constitution of the United States of America

The first ten Amendments to the Constitution, the

BILL OF RIGHTS

were ratified effective December 15, 1791.

Amendment 1

Congress shall make no law respecting an establishment of religion, or prohibiting the free exercise thereof; or abridging the freedom of speech, or of the press; or the right of the people peaceably to assemble, and to petition the Government for a redress of grievances.

Amendment 2

A well regulated Militia, being necessary to the security of a free State, the right of the people to keep and bear Arms, shall not be infringed.

Amendment 3

No Soldier shall, in time of peace be quartered in any house, without the consent of the Owner, nor in time of war, but in a manner to be prescribed by law.

Amendment 4

The right of the people to be secure in their persons, houses, papers, and effects, against unreasonable searches and seizures, shall not be violated, and no Warrants shall issue, but upon probable cause, supported by Oath or affirmation, and particularly describing the place to be searched, and the persons or things to be seized.

Amendment 5

No person shall be held to answer for a capital, or otherwise infamous crime, unless on a presentment or indictment of a Grand Jury, except in cases arising in the land or naval forces, or in the Militia, when in actual service in time of War or public danger; nor shall any person be subject for the same offense to be twice put in jeopardy of life or limb; nor shall be compelled in any criminal case to be a witness against himself, nor be deprived of life, liberty, or property, without due process of law; nor shall private property be taken for public use, without just compensation.

Amendment 6

In all criminal prosecutions, the accused shall enjoy the right to a speedy and public trial, by an impartial jury of the State and district wherein the crime shall have been committed, which district shall have been previously ascertained by law, and to be informed of the nature and cause of the accusation; to be confronted with the witnesses against him; to have compulsory process for obtaining witnesses in his favor, and to have the Assistance of Counsel for his defence.

Amendment 7

In Suits at common law, where the value in controversy shall exceed twenty dollars, the right of trial by jury shall be preserved, and no fact tried by a jury, shall be otherwise re-examined in any Court of the United States, than according to the rules of the common law.

Amendment 8

Excessive bail shall not be required, nor excessive fines imposed, nor cruel and unusual punishments inflicted.

Amendment 9

The enumeration in the Constitution, of certain rights, shall not be construed to deny or disparage others retained by the people.

Amendment 10

The powers not delegated to the United States by the Constitution, nor prohibited by it to the States, are reserved to the States respectively, or to the people.

Amendment 11

Ratified February 7, 1795

The Judicial power of the United States shall not be construed to extend to any suit in law or equity, commenced or prosecuted against one of the United States by Citizens of another State, or by Citizens or Subjects of any Foreign State.

Amendment 12

Ratified June 15, 1804

The Electors shall meet in their respective states, and vote by ballot for President and Vice-President, one of whom, at least, shall not be an inhabitant of the same state with themselves; they shall name in their ballots the person voted for as President, and in distinct ballots the person voted for as Vice-President, and they shall make distinct lists of all persons voted for as President, and of all persons voted for as Vice-President and of the number of votes for each, which lists they shall sign and certify, and transmit sealed to the seat of the government of the United States, directed to the President of the Senate;

The President of the Senate shall, in the presence of the Senate and House of Representatives, open all the certificates and the votes shall then be counted;

The person having the greatest Number of votes for President, shall be the President, if such number be a majority of the whole number of Electors appointed; and if no person have such majority, then from the persons having the highest numbers not exceeding three on the list of those voted for as President, the House of Representatives shall choose immediately, by ballot, the President. But in choosing the President, the votes shall be taken by states, the representation from each state having one vote; a quorum for this purpose shall consist of a member or members from two-thirds of the states, and a majority of all the states shall be necessary to a choice. And if the House of Representatives shall not choose a President whenever the right of choice shall devolve upon them, before the fourth day of March next following, then the Vice-President shall act as President, as in the case of the death or other constitutional disability of the President.

The person having the greatest number of votes as Vice-President, shall be the Vice-President, if such number be a majority of the whole number of Electors appointed, and if no person have a majority, then from the two highest numbers on the list, the Senate shall choose the Vice-President; a quorum for the purpose shall consist of two-thirds of the whole number of Senators, and a majority of the whole number shall be necessary to a choice. But no person constitutionally ineligible to the office of President shall be eligible to that of Vice-President of the United States.

Amendment 13
Ratified December 6, 1865

1.Neither slavery nor involuntary servitude, except as a punishment for crime whereof the party shall have been duly convicted, shall exist within the United States, or any place subject to their jurisdiction.
2. Congress shall have power to enforce this article by appropriate legislation.

Amendment 14
Ratified July 9, 1868

1. All persons born or naturalized in the United States, and subject to the jurisdiction thereof, are citizens of the United States and of the State wherein they reside. No State shall make or enforce any law which shall abridge the privileges or immunities of citizens of the United States; nor shall any State deprive any person of life, liberty, or property, without due process of law; nor deny to any person within its jurisdiction the equal protection of the laws.

2. Representatives shall be apportioned among the several States according to their respective numbers, counting the whole number of persons in each State, excluding Indians not taxed. But when the right to vote at any election for the choice of electors for President and Vice-President of the United States, Representatives in Congress, the Executive and Judicial officers of a State, or the members of the Legislature thereof, is denied to any of the male inhabitants of such State, being twenty-one years of age, and citizens of the United States, or in any way abridged, except for participation in rebellion, or other crime, the basis of representation therein shall be reduced in the proportion which the number of such male citizens shall bear to the whole number of male citizens twenty-one years of age in such State.

3. No person shall be a Senator or Representative in Congress, or elector of President and Vice-President, or hold any office, civil or military, under the United States, or under any State, who, having previously taken an oath, as a member of Congress, or as an officer of the United States, or as a member of any State legislature, or as an executive or judicial officer of any State, to support the Constitution of the United States, shall have engaged in insurrection or rebellion against the same, or given aid or comfort to the enemies thereof. But Congress may by a vote of two-thirds of each House, remove such disability.

4. The validity of the public debt of the United States, authorized by law, including debts incurred for payment of pensions and bounties for services in suppressing insurrection or rebellion, shall not be questioned. But neither the United States nor any State shall assume or pay any debt or obligation incurred in aid of insurrection or

rebellion against the United States, or any claim for the loss or emancipation of any slave; but all such debts, obligations and claims shall be held illegal and void.

5. The Congress shall have power to enforce, by appropriate legislation, the provisions of this article.

Amendment 15

Ratified February 3, 1870

1. The right of citizens of the United States to vote shall not be denied or abridged by the United States or by any State on account of race, color, or previous condition of servitude.

2. The Congress shall have power to enforce this article by appropriate legislation.

Amendment 16

Ratified February 3, 1913

The Congress shall have power to lay and collect taxes on incomes, from whatever source derived, without apportionment among the several States, and without regard to any census or enumeration.

Amendment 17

Ratified April 8, 1913

The Senate of the United States shall be composed of two Senators from each State, elected by the people thereof, for six years; and each Senator shall have one vote. The electors in each State shall have the qualifications requisite for electors of the most numerous branch of the State legislatures.

When vacancies happen in the representation of any

State in the Senate, the executive authority of such State shall issue writs of election to fill such vacancies: Provided, That the legislature of any State may empower the executive thereof to make temporary appointments until the people fill the vacancies by election as the legislature may direct.

This amendment shall not be so construed as to affect the election or term of any Senator chosen before it becomes valid as part of the Constitution.

Amendment 18

Ratified January 16, 1919

1. After one year from the ratification of this article the manufacture, sale, or transportation of intoxicating liquors within, the importation thereof into, or the exportation thereof from the United States and all territory subject to the jurisdiction thereof for beverage purposes is hereby prohibited.
2. The Congress and the several States shall have concurrent power to enforce this article by appropriate legislation.
3. This article shall be inoperative unless it shall have been ratified as an amendment to the Constitution by the legislatures of the several States, as provided in the Constitution, within seven years from the date of the submission hereof to the States by the Congress.

Amendment 19

Ratified August 18, 1920

The right of citizens of the United States to vote shall not be denied or abridged by the United States or by any State on account of sex.

Congress shall have power to enforce this article by appropriate legislation.

Amendment 20

Ratified January 23, 1933

1. The terms of the President and Vice President shall end at noon on the 20th day of January, and the terms of Senators and Representatives at noon on the 3d day of January, of the years in which such terms would have ended if this article had not been ratified; and the terms of their successors shall then begin.

2. The Congress shall assemble at least once in every year, and such meeting shall begin at noon on the 3d day of January, unless they shall by law appoint a different day.

3. If, at the time fixed for the beginning of the term of the President, the President elect shall have died, the Vice President elect shall become President. If a President shall not have been chosen before the time fixed for the beginning of his term, or if the President elect shall have failed to qualify, then the Vice President elect shall act as President until a President shall have qualified; and the Congress may by law provide for the case wherein neither a President elect nor a Vice President elect shall have qualified, declaring who shall then act as President, or the manner in which one who is to act shall be selected, and such person shall act accordingly until a President or Vice President shall have qualified.

4. The Congress may by law provide for the case of the death of any of the persons from whom the House of Representatives may choose a President whenever the right of choice shall have devolved upon them, and for the case of the death of any of the persons from whom the Senate may choose a Vice President whenever the right of choice shall have devolved upon them.

5. Sections 1 and 2 shall take effect on the 15th day of

October following the ratification of this article.

6. This article shall be inoperative unless it shall have been ratified as an amendment to the Constitution by the legislatures of three-fourths of the several States within seven years from the date of its submission.

Amendment 21

Ratified December 5, 1933

1. The eighteenth article of amendment to the Constitution of the United States is hereby repealed.

2. The transportation or importation into any State, Territory, or possession of the United States for delivery or use therein of intoxicating liquors, in violation of the laws thereof, is hereby prohibited.

3. The article shall be inoperative unless it shall have been ratified as an amendment to the Constitution by conventions in the several States, as provided in the Constitution, within seven years from the date of the submission hereof to the States by the Congress.

Amendment 22

Ratified February 27, 1951

1. No person shall be elected to the office of the President more than twice, and no person who has held the office of President, or acted as President, for more than two years of a term to which some other person was elected President shall be elected to the office of the President more than once. But this Article shall not apply to any person holding the office of President, when this Article was proposed by the Congress, and shall not prevent any person who may be holding the office of President, or acting as President, during the term within which this Article becomes

operative from holding the office of President or acting as President during the remainder of such term.

2. This article shall be inoperative unless it shall have been ratified as an amendment to the Constitution by the legislatures of three-fourths of the several States within seven years from the date of its submission to the States by the Congress.

Amendment 23

Ratified March 29, 1961

1. The District constituting the seat of Government of the United States shall appoint in such manner as the Congress may direct:

A number of electors of President and Vice President equal to the whole number of Senators and Representatives in Congress to which the District would be entitled if it were a State, but in no event more than the least populous State; they shall be in addition to those appointed by the States, but they shall be considered, for the purposes of the election of President and Vice President, to be electors appointed by a State; and they shall meet in the District and perform such duties as provided by the twelfth article of amendment.

2. The Congress shall have power to enforce this article by appropriate legislation.

Amendment 24

Ratified January 23, 1964

1. The right of citizens of the United States to vote in any primary or other election for President or Vice President, for electors for President or Vice President, or for Senator or Representative in Congress, shall not be denied or

abridged by the United States or any State by reason of failure to pay any poll tax or other tax.

2. The Congress shall have power to enforce this article by appropriate legislation.

Amendment 25

Ratified February 10, 1967

1. In case of the removal of the President from office or of his death or resignation, the Vice President shall become President.

2. Whenever there is a vacancy in the office of the Vice President, the President shall nominate a Vice President who shall take office upon confirmation by a majority vote of both Houses of Congress.

3. Whenever the President transmits to the President pro tempore of the Senate and the Speaker of the House of Representatives his written declaration that he is unable to discharge the powers and duties of his office, and until he transmits to them a written declaration to the contrary, such powers and duties shall be discharged by the Vice President as Acting President.

4. Whenever the Vice President and a majority of either the principal officers of the executive departments or of such other body as Congress may by law provide, transmit to the President pro tempore of the Senate and the Speaker of the House of Representatives their written declaration that the President is unable to discharge the powers and duties of his office, the Vice President shall immediately assume the powers and duties of the office as Acting President.

Thereafter, when the President transmits to the President pro tempore of the Senate and the Speaker of the House of Representatives his written declaration that no inability exists, he shall resume the powers and duties of his office unless the Vice President and a majority of either the principal officers of the executive department or of such other body as Congress may by law provide, transmit within four days to the President pro tempore of the Senate and the Speaker of the House of Representatives their written declaration that the President is unable to discharge the powers and duties of his office. Thereupon Congress shall decide the issue, assembling within forty eight hours for that purpose if not in session. If the Congress, within twenty one days after receipt of the latter written declaration, or, if Congress is not in session, within twenty one days after Congress is required to assemble, determines by two thirds vote of both Houses that the President is unable to discharge the powers and duties of his office, the Vice President shall continue to discharge the same as Acting President; otherwise, the President shall resume the powers and duties of his office.

Amendment 26

Ratified July 1, 1971

1. The right of citizens of the United States, who are eighteen years of age or older, to vote shall not be denied or abridged by the United States or by any State on account of age.
2. The Congress shall have power to enforce this article by appropriate legislation.

Amendment 27

Ratified May 7, 1992

No law, varying the compensation for the services of the Senators and Representatives, shall take effect, until an election of Representatives shall have intervened.

HISTORICAL BASICS

Purpose: To provide for the common defense, protect human rights, establish a representative form of government.

Framers: Delegates from the original thirteen states

Parchment: Four sheets 28-3/4 in. by 23-5/8 in. each

Words: 4,448 (4,543 including signatures)
7,591 including the 27 amendments

Articles: 7

Amendments: 27

Constitutional Convention: May 25 - September 17, 1787, in the Pennsylvania State House, now Independence Hall

Signers: 55 total signers, 55 total delegates
42 delegates usually attended the Convention
39 delegates actually signed on September 17, 1787
3 delegates did not sign until there was a bill of rights.

Constitution is officially established on June 21, 1788

Remaining states that joined afterward: Virginia (June 25, 1788), New York (July 26, 1788), North Carolina (November 21, 1789), Rhode Island (May 29, 1790)

Time to Ratify: 9 months from signing to ninth state ratifying

Signed: September 17, 1787

Ratified: June 21, 1788

First Congress seated: March 4, 1789

First President seated: George Washington, April 30, 1789

Supreme Court convenes: February 2, 1790

Second President seated: John Adams, March 4, 1797

Nine States to Ratify:

Delaware—December 7, 1787

Pennsylvania—December 12, 1787

New Jersey—December 18, 1787

Georgia—January 2, 1788

Connecticut—January 9, 1788

Massachusetts—February 6, 1788

Maryland—April 28, 1788

South Carolina—May 23, 1788

New Hampshire—June 21, 1788

IMPORTANT DATES

April 19, 1775: Battle of Lexington, War for Independence starts.

July 4, 1776: Declaration of Independence adopted by Congress.

November 15, 1777: Articles of Confederation created.

March 1, 1781: Articles of Confederation ratitifed.

October 19, 1781: Cornwallis surrenders at Yorktown, ending British military action and the war.

September 3, 1783: Treaty of Paris signed. Great Britain recognizes colonists' independence.

May 25, 1787: The Constitutional Convention opens in Philadelphia to discuss revising the Articles of Confederation.

July 13, 1787: Congress passes the Northwest Ordinance.

September 17, 1787: All 12 state delegations approve the Constitution. and the Convention formally adjourns.

June 21, 1788: The Constitution becomes effective for the ratifying states when New Hampshire is the 9th state to ratify.

March 4, 1789: The first Congress under the Constitution convenes in New York City.

April 30, 1789: George Washington is inaugurated as the first president of the United States.

June 8, 1789: James Madison introduced proposed Bill of Rights in the House of Representatives.

September 24, 1789: Congress establishes a Supreme Court, 13 district courts, three ad hoc circuit courts, and the position of Attorney General.

September 25, 1789: Congress approves 12 Amendments and sends them to the states for ratification.

February 2, 1790: Supreme Court convenes for the first time after an unsuccessful attempt February 1.

December 15, 1791: Virginia ratifies the Bill of Rights, and 10 of the 12 proposed Amendments become part of the Constitution.

TEN POPULAR MYTHS

Misunderstandings about the Constitution

1. *Myth*—**The Constitution is Old Fashioned**
Response: **Protecting unalienable rights won't grow old.** We all wonder—is it "old fashioned"? If so, the next question must be, "which part?" The Constitution controls the political powers that protect our rights. Changing those privileges and constraints exposes our rights to political abuse and eventual destruction.

2. *Myth*—**It's a Living Document; It Must Change**
Response: We all wonder—shouldn't it "change with the times"? The power of the Constitution to protect human rights never depended on our culture, economics, technology, or world affairs. It stands apart to ensure that our rights do not succumb to the shifting priorities of passing generations. So long as the people want their human rights protected, the Constitution must remain an uncompromising, unchanging defender against all challengers.

3. *Myth*—**Executive Orders Are the Law**
Response: The number of Executive Orders doesn't matter, but their content does. Presidents using them to make new laws defy the proper and lawful role of Congress.

4. *Myth*—It's a Complicated Document

Response: The Constitution was written so that all Americans could understand it. Spending time to read and study it will bring increased insight into how all Americans may better unite to strengthen and support each other.

5. *Myth*—Disruption is Protected Free Speech

Response: The First Amendment protects a speaker's right to speak and the listeners' right to listen. Hecklers who shout down speakers or disrupt proceedings illegally violate the rights of everyone present who came to both speak and to be spoken to.

6. *Myth*—Supreme Court Interprets the Constitution

Response: The actual text of the Constitution is the "supreme Law of the Land." The Court is not authorized to interpret or use prior interpretations to resolve legal issues. The Justices are supposed to apply original intent and meaning, not interpret to achieve different meanings. Thomas Jefferson saw that abuse coming and warned there should have been a check and balance placed on the Court.

7. *Myth*—Prayer Was Legally Banned from Schools

Response: Originally the States were empowered to set their own rules on religion, not Congress. In 1962 the Supreme Court transformed that state role into a federal role by banning prayer and Bible study in all public schools.

8. *Myth*—The Bill of Rights Lists Our Human Rights

Response: Every human right existed before the Constitution. The Bill of Rights is not an exhaustive list of all rights but does list several specific human rights the government may not abuse or abolish.

9. *Myth*—It's a Hodgepodge of Compromises

Response: There were only three main compromises: Slavery could continue for 20 years if the South would join the union; the federal government could regulate interstate trade; and state representation would include Representatives based on population, and two Senators per state. All other issues were debated and passed by majority vote.

10. *Myth*—Federal Government Controls the States

Response: The States must obey every Congressional law that does not violate the Constitution. If a new law is unconstitutional the States are free to disregard it without waiting on the Supreme Court's examination.

GLOSSARY

The following words may have more than one meaning. This list only includes definitions that pertain to the Constitution and the Declaration of Independence. For more detailed definitions of these words as they were understood in the late 1700s, see Noah Webster's "American Dictionary of the English Language," 1828.

ABDICATED – gave up a right, responsibility, or duty

ABSOLVED – set free or released

ACCOMMODATION – the process of adapting or adjusting to someone or something

ACQUIESCE – to agree without protest

ADHERING – being attached as a follower

ADJOURN – to postpone action of a convened legislative body until another time specified

ADMIRALTY AND MARITIME LAW – laws relating to the sea, lakes, and rivers.

ADMIT – to allow

AFFECTED – influenced, aspired to, sought to obtain

AFFIRMATION – declaration, confirmation or ratification that something is true

ALLEGIANCE – loyalty or devotion to a group, person, or cause

AMBASSADOR – an authorized messenger or representative

AMENDMENT – a formal alteration or addition to the United States Constitution.

ANNIHILATION – being destroyed or wiped out completely

APPEAL – to request from some person or authority a decision, reconsideration, judgment; to attract, interest, amuse

APPELLATE – relating to appeals, which are reviews of lower court decisions by a higher court

APPLICATION – a formal request to an authority

APPORTION – give out in portions, divided, allocated, distribute according to a plan; set apart for a special purpose

ARBITRARY – unrestricted, not according to set laws, at the whim of someone else such as a king

ARSENALS – places for making or storing weapons and munitions

ARTICLE – a section or part of a written document

ASCERTAINED – established

ASSEMBLE – to bring together or gather into one place

ASSENT – consent or agreement

ASSUME – to take on, to take over, to take for granted

AT LARGE – free; free roaming; un-captured; in general

ATTAINDER – a law that declares a person an outlaw or criminal without a formal trial; removal of civil rights and property without trial; used to confiscate property of political enemies

ATTAINTED – a French term meaning "touched" by the finger of accusation

BAIL – money given to guarantee a person released from custody will return at an appointed time. If the person fails to return, the money is given up.

BALLOT – a document on which a voter marks a vote

BANDS – things that bind or unite

BENEFICENT – causing good to be done

BILL OF ATTAINDER – a law passed against a person that pronounces him guilty without a trial by jury

BILL OF RIGHTS – the first ten Amendments to the Constitution that were adopted in 1791. They list several human rights the federal government may not disturb.

BILL – a proposed law that is presented for discussion and approval; also, a list of items such as the Bill of Rights

BLESSINGS – favors, mercies, or benefits

BOUNTIES – rewards for performing certain acts for the government such as joining the military

BREACH – violation, disturbance

BRETHREN – associates or peers closely united or connected

BRITAIN, GREAT BRITAIN – before 1707, Britain included England and Wales. In 1707, Scotland joined to create Great Britain. Both terms mean the islands and political union shared by England, Scotland and Wales.

CANDID – transparent; free from prejudice; fair or impartial

CAPITAL – punishable by death

CAPITATION – a poll tax, head tax, uniform amount for each person

CASES – instances; matters to be decided in a court of law

CENSUS – a count of the population

CERTIFICATES – a written and signed document serving as evidence to the truth of facts stated

CERTIFY – make a declaration in writing

CESSION – the act of transferring the title of ownership, such as ceding land to become the seat of government

CHARTER – a document outlining the conditions under which a colony is organized

CHECKS AND BALANCES – "check" means to stop or prevent; "balance" means equal with the others. It's a system set up by the Constitution giving power to the executive, legislative, and judicial branches of government to prevent each other from overreach, and to maintain a "balance" of power.

CHIEF JUSTICE – the senior judge of the Supreme Court

CIVIL – relating to citizens in their ordinary capacity in a community as separate from their role in military, government, or ecclesiastical service

COLONY – a group of people who settle an area away from their homeland, but remain under the political control of their homeland

COMMANDER IN CHIEF – supreme commander of the armed forces

COMMISSION – a written document authorizing a person to perform certain duties; the act of giving a commission

COMMON LAW – that body of ancient and modern rules, Principles, and customs recognized by courts as the law of the land. Not the same as "statutory law," which are laws made by legislatures. (see *People's Law, Ruler's Law*)

COMPACT – contract or treaty

COMPENSATION – amends for service or injury; payment for service

COMPULSORY PROCESS – a legal document ordering a person to appear in court

CONCLUDE – to make a final determination

CONCUR – to agree

CONCURRENCE – agreement

CONCURRENT – existing, occurring, or operating at the same time

CONFEDERATION – a group of independent nations or states joined together. "Confederation" referred to the United States before the Constitution was adopted.

CONGRESS – the legislature of the United States government. The U.S. Congress includes the Senate and House of Representatives. Also, a congress is a meeting of people dealing with issues important to their common good

CONJURED – asked earnestly; brought to mind

CONSENT – permission

CONSTITUTING – forming

CONSTITUTION – from the Latin "constitutio," the regulations and orders to establish or to fix what a government is, what it does, and its laws and principles. A written constitution is far more powerful than an oral or assumed understanding. The U.S. Constitution was written at the Constitutional Convention in Philadelphia in 1787 and later ratified by the original thirteen states.

CONSTITUTIONALLY – according to the constitution

CONSTRAINS – forces or compels

CONSTRUED – interpreted or explained; assigned a meaning to something

CONSUL – an official appointed by the government of one country to look after the commercial interests and welfare of its citizens in another country.

CONTROVERSIES – lawsuits

CONVENE – to come together or assemble

CONVENTION – formal meeting of delegates or representatives

CORRESPONDENCE – communication

CORRUPTION OF BLOOD – considering a person guilty of the same crime as a guilty relative, and disqualifying the person from inheriting or retaining the guilty person's properties.

CREDIT – faith and confidence in the ability of others to perform on their promises, such as to repay borrowed money

CROWN – the power of a king

DECENT – fit or suitable

DECLARATION – a public announcement

DECLARE – to state that a person or thing exists in a certain way

DEEM – conclude

DELEGATED POWERS – the 20 powers that are exclusively for the federal government. They are listed in Article I, Section 8.

DEMOCRACY – a government run directly by the people where there are no representatives: "one man, one vote." This works at the lowest levels of government, but after that, representatives are far more efficient in governing the affairs of the nation.

DENOUNCES – proclaims in a threatening or accusing manner

DENY – to refuse to recognize

DEPOSITORY – a place where anything is kept for safekeeping

DEPRIVE – to take away

DESIGN – plan or purpose

DESPOTISM – absolute power or control, tyranny

DEVOLVE – to pass down duties from one person to another at a lower level, such as from president to vice president

DISAVOW – to repudiate or condemn

DISCIPLINE – a level of education or instruction set by Congress

DISPARAGE – to regard as being of little worth

DISPOSE OF – to deal with or settle

DISPOSED – tending or inclined to do or to be something

DISTINCT – separate

DISTRICT – an area of a country or city

DOMESTIC TRANQUILITY – peace at home

DOMESTIC – local, or refers to one's own country

DUE PROCESS OF LAW – the regular administration of justice according to the established rule of laws

DULY – properly, fittingly, at the proper time

DUTY – a payment due to the government such as taxes on imports and exports; that which a person is bound by natural or moral obligation to perform

EFFECT – to produce or cause

EFFECTS – personal belongings

EITHER – one or the other

ELECT – to choose; to select from among others by vote

ELECTOR – a citizen who elects or who has a legal right to vote

ELECTOR – a person who votes at the Electoral College for president and vice president

ELECTORAL COLLEGE – the group of people who elect the president and vice president

ELIGIBLE – qualified, worthy, or allowed

EMANCIPATION – the act of freeing someone from slavery

EMIT – to print or issue and put formally into circulation with authority

EMOLUMENT – compensation for services; salary, wages, fees

ENDOWED – provided with a quality or power

ENDS – the intended purposes

ENFORCE – compel to behave in a certain way

ENGAGEMENTS – obligations by agreement or contract

ENJOY – to have, possess, and use with satisfaction

ENTANGLING – interlocking in confusion, ensnaring

ENTITLE – to give the right to

ENUMERATION – establishing the number of something

EQUITY – impartial distribution of justice

ESTABLISH – to set up on a permanent basis

EVINCES – to show in a clear manner, to prove beyond reasonable doubt

EX POST FACTO LAW – "after the fact." A law that makes an action a crime after it was committed. Latin, "from a thing done afterward."

EXCISE – a tax on the manufacture, sale, or consumption of various commodities such as liquor, tobacco, etc.

EXCITED – created or caused, as in, "He has excited domestic insurrections"

EXECUTION – the putting into operation

EXECUTIVE BRANCH – one of the three branches of the U.S. government with the purpose of enforcing laws

EXECUTIVE DEPARTMENTS – these are departments in the executive branch such as the Departments of Defense, Commerce and Agriculture. Today there are 15 departments.

EXERCISE – performance of duties

EXPEDIENT – proper under the circumstances

EXPORTATION – the selling and shipping of goods to another state or to a foreign country

FAITH – belief; confidence; trust

FATIGUING – to weaken by harassing

FEDERAL – the central government in league with cooperative states

FELONY – a major crime such as murder, arson, rape, etc.

FIT – convenient

FORFEITURE – losing rights, privileges, property, honor, or office as a penalty or payment for a crime

FORMIDABLE – feared or dreaded

FREE PERSON – someone who is not a slave

FREE – independent and able to think or act without restriction

FULL FAITH AND CREDIT CLAUSE – from Article IV, it means that all states are required to honor the laws, judgments, and public documents of every other state

GENERAL – concerning all or most people

GOVERNMENT – a body that governs; or, the act of direction or controlling

GRAND JURY – a grand jury is a jury that investigates allegations of a crime and issues indictments if it finds there is sufficient evidence against the person or persons

GROUND – foundation; beginning; that which supports anything

HABEAS CORPUS – Latin for "have the body." A writ of habeas corpus is a legal document ordering the delivery of a person from false imprisonment; or, his delivery to a court to decide on the legality of his imprisonment.

HAPPINESS – from Noah Webster, 1828: "The agreeable sensations which spring from the enjoyment of good; that state of a being in which his desires are gratified, by the enjoyment of pleasure without pain; ... indefinite degrees of increase in enjoyment, or gratification of desires. Perfect happiness, or pleasure unalloyed with pain, is not attainable in this life."

HEREIN – in this document

HIGH CRIMES – acts against the public morality that are great but technically are not a felony; or, crimes punishable by death

HIGH SEAS – the open ocean not under the jurisdiction of a country

HITHER – to this place

HOUSE OF REPRESENTATIVES – the "lower" house of Congress in which states are represented based on population. Presently there are 435 members in the House.

HUMBLE – submissive

IMMUNITIES – freedoms

IMMUTABLE – unchanging over time or unable to be changed

IMPEACHMENT – the accusation, charge, or indictment before an appropriate tribunal of misconduct in office; a constitutional "check" the Congress has on the President or other high federal officials. It involves an accusation against that official by the House, and removal from office, or other punishment if found guilty of the impeachment by the Senate.

IMPEL – to drive or urge forward

IMPORTATION – buying of goods from another country

IMPOST – a tax, especially a tax on imported goods

IN GENERAL – relating to or including all members

IN CONSEQUENCE – as a result

INALIENABLE RIGHTS – the natural rights of all men, defined by John Locke as life, liberty, and property; can only be taken away by God. Government is created to protect these rights. Also spelled *un*alienable.

INDICTMENT – a formal written charge against one or more people presented to a court

INESTIMABLE – too valuable or precious to be properly measured or estimated

INEVITABLY – unavoidably

INFAMOUS CRIME – a crime which is punishable by imprisonment or death

INFERIOR OFFICERS – government officials of lower rank than ambassadors, Supreme Court justices, etc.

INOPERATIVE – not working or taking effect

INSTITUTED – set up, established, organized

INSTRUMENT – someone or something used as a means for accomplishing a specific purpose

INSURRECTION – organized opposition to authority

INSURRECTIONS – violent uprisings against authority or government

INTERVENE – to come between disputing people; to intercede

INTOXICATING – making drunk (with alcoholic drinks)

INVESTED – provided with something

INVOLUNTARY SERVITUDE – a slave-like condition. Sometimes British criminals were sold to American colonists to labor for them during the term of their sentence.

JUDICIAL REVIEW – a power the Supreme Court conferred upon itself in the 1803 case of Marbury v. Madison (1803) to review the constitutionality of acts passed by Congress or actions by the president

JUDICIAL BRANCH – one of the three branches of our government assigned to interpret the laws

JUDICIAL – refers to judges, courts, or their functions

JUDICIARY – dealing with courts of law

JUNCTION – act of joining, such as two states to make one

JURISDICTION – the power to govern, to make, declare or apply the law; the territory within which power can be exercised

JUST – honest; conforming to moral and proper principles of social conduct

JUSTICE – from Noah Webster, 1828: "The virtue which consists in giving to every one what is his due; practical conformity to the laws and principles of rectitude in the dealings of men with each other."

KINDRED – related by blood

LAID – imposed as a burden or penalty

LAW OF NATIONS – from Noah Webster, 1828: "The rules that regulate the mutual intercourse of nations or states. These rules depend on natural law, or the principles of justice which spring from the social state..."

LAW – rules established by governments for regulating people's actions

LAWS OF NATURE – from Noah Webster, 1828: "a rule of conduct arising out of the natural relations of human beings established by the Creator, and existing prior to any positive precept. Thus it is a law of nature, that one man should not injure another, and murder and fraud would be crimes, independent of any prohibition from a supreme power."

LAY – to set or impose (to lay and collect taxes)

LEGISLATIVE – referring to the power to make laws

LEGISLATURE – people who make or amend or repeal laws

LETTERS OF MARQUE AND REPRISAL – from Noah Webster, 1828: "a commission granted by a supreme authority of a state to a subject, empowering him to pass the frontiers [marque] that is, enter an enemy's territories and capture the goods and persons of the enemy, in return for goods and persons taken by him." See Reprisal.

LEVYING – collecting money for public use by tax; collecting soldiers for military or other public service by enlistment

LIBERTY – from Noah Webster, 1828: "Freedom from restraint, in a general sense, and applicable to the body, or to the will or mind; the power to act as one thinks fit, without any restraint or control, except from the laws of nature; freedom of a nation or state from all unjust abridgment of its rights and independence by another nation."

LIFE – the condition in which a human being's natural functions and motions are performed. In mankind, that state of being in which the spirit, intellect, and body are united we identify as life.

MAGAZINES – places of storage or military supply depots

MAGNANIMITY – the quality of being noble and generous in one's conduct and rising above pettiness or meanness

MAJORITY – more than half; the main part

MANLY – brave

MEASURES – inches, feet, yards, etc.; also, actions to be taken

MERCENARIES – hired soldiers

MILITIA – body of soldiers organized from the civilian population in times of emergencies

MISCONSTRUCTION – mistaking the true meaning

MISDEMEANORS – offenses less serious than crimes

MOCK – to imitate or mimic in contempt or derision; to deride

MODE – manner; method

NATIVE – conferred by birth, produced by nature

NATURALIZATION – the granting to a person of foreign

birth the rights of citizenship in a new country

NATURALIZE – to make into a citizen

NATURAL LAW – a law that is discoverable by reason, based on right reason, of universal application, and is unchanging and everlasting. Natural Law brings about cooperative harmony and is basic in its principles; it is comprehensible to the human mind and protects human rights; it guides the creation of all moral laws.

NAY – a "no" vote

NET – to produce a clear profit after all deductions have been made

NOMINATE – to propose as a candidate for some honor

NOTWITHSTANDING – without being affected by the particular factor mentioned

OATH – a formal declaration with an appeal to God for the truth of what is being declared

OBJECT – aim or goal

OFFICE – a particular duty or employment

OFFICERS – persons commissioned or authorized to perform a public duty.

OPERATIVE – producing a desired effect

ORDAIN – officially order

ORIGINAL JURISDICTION – the authority to try a case from its beginning

OTHER OFFICERS – people appointed to positions of responsibility in the government

OTHER PUBLIC MINISTERS – government officials sent to represent their own government in another country and ranking below an ambassador

OVERT ACT – the act of committing a crime that is open to view

PARALLELED – equaled

PARDON – lessening or setting aside the punishment for a crime

PEACE – a state of quiet or tranquility; freedom from disturbance or agitation; freedom from war or internal commotion; that quiet, order and security which is guaranteed by the laws

PEOPLE – the group of people who make up a nation

PEOPLE'S LAW – natural law; self-rule, self-government: all decisions and selection of leaders are done with consent of the people, laws must comply with natural law, power is dispersed among the people, resolving problems happens on local level, every adult has a voice and a vote, rights are unalienable, government has no more rights than the people themselves have, government's rights are delegated rights

PERFIDY – treachery

PETITIONED – made a formal request

POLITICAL – relating to government or public affairs

POLL TAX – a tax of a fixed amount per person and payable before they may vote ("poll" means a person's head)

POST ROADS – roads over which mail is carried

POSTERITY – all of a person's descendants; all future generations or future mankind

POWERS – rights and authorities; influential countries. Powers reserved to the states are identified in the Tenth Amendment.

PREJUDICE – to hurt, damage, or dismiss

PRESCRIBE – to lay down rules; to order or direct

PRESENTMENT – a report made by a grand jury of an offense that the grand jury observed or learned during their investigations

PRESIDENT PRO TEMPORE – the senior member of the majority party in the Senate who serves as the president of the Senate when the Vice President is absent

PRESIDENT – the person who holds the office of head of state of the United States government

PRIVILEGED – enjoying a peculiar right or immunity

PRO TEMPORE – temporary, for the time being

PROBABLE CAUSE – a valid reason in presuming someone is guilty of some illegal act

PRODUCE – yield or product, as in "the net Produce of all Duties and Imposts"

PROHIBIT – to command against

PROVIDE – to make available for use; to make adequate preparation; to enable or allow

PROVIDED – "provided" is used in legal documents to introduce a condition or requirement

PROVIDENCE – God or the protective care of nature as a spiritual power

PRUDENCE – good judgment

PUBLIC DOMAIN – the lands held by the state or the federal government

PUBLIC – in open view

PUBLISH – to formally announce

PURSUANCE – the carrying out of something in the way that is expected or required

QUARTERING – lodging

QUORUM – the minimum number of members of a group required to be present to make the actions of that assembly valid

RATIFICATION – making valid by formally confirming

RATIFIED – formally approved and invested with legal authority

RATIFY – to give formal approval to something

RECESS – suspension of business

RECTITUDE – correctness of behavior

REDRESS – the setting right of what is wrong; satisfaction or compensation for a wrong or injury

RENDER – to cause to be; to make, perform, furnish, provide, exhibit

REPRESENTATIVE – a person who acts on behalf of the voters or a community in a legislative body

REPRIEVES – postponements of punishments

REPRISAL – from Noah Webster, 1828: to capture "the goods and persons of the enemy, in return for goods and persons taken by him." See *Letters of Marque and Reprisal*.

REPUBLIC – the type of government in which voters elect

representatives to make the laws for the country.

REQUISITE – required or necessary for relief or supply

RESERVING – retaining, keeping back, saving for another

RESIGNATION – the act of giving up an office or position

RESOLUTION – formal expression of opinion or intention by a legislature

RESPECT – that positive view or honor in which we hold the good qualities of others; to give regard, good will, favor

RESPECTING – regarding, in view of, considering

RESPECTIVELY – separately or individually

RETURNS – reports on the count of votes at polling places

RHODE ISLAND AND PROVIDENCE PLANTATIONS – the name of four early settlements in what is now Rhode Island

RIGHT – from Noah Webster, 1828: "Conformity to the will of God or to his law, the perfect standard of truth and justice"; a power, privilege, moral or legal claim which correctly belongs to a person by law, by nature, or by tradition; to correct a wrong; to restore to normal or correct condition

RULER'S LAW – rule by the king where all power and rights are in the king, for example: people are not equal, all property is ruler's, power is from top down, no unalienable rights, ruled by whim of the ruler, no fixed rule of law, ruler issues edicts that are law, freedom never considered a solution

SEAT – site of the national government; place of official capacity

SECURE – make certain; not exposed to danger, in safe custody

SECURITIES – investments that are easily bought or sold

SEDITION – attempt to overthrow or interrupt a government

SELF-EVIDENT – plain or obvious in itself without additional proof

SENATE – one of the two houses of Congress (the "upper" house) with two representatives from each state. Presently there are 100 senators.

SERVITUDE – slavery or bondage to an owner or master

SEVERAL – individual, separate, or distinct

SITTING – present to perform its business

SOVEREIGN – independent, holding all power and authority

SPEAKER OF THE HOUSE – the presiding officer of the U.S. House of Representatives

SPEAKER – the officer presiding over a lawmaking body, such as the House of Representatives

STANDING – status, permanently in existence

STATES' RIGHTS – all rights not delegated to the federal government or denied to the states

STATION – position or rank

STRICT INTERPRETATION – interpreting the Constitution based on its literal words, meaning, and intention

SUBSCRIBED – attested by signing at the end of a document

SUBSTANCE – means of living; also the matter of which things consist

SUCCESSOR – that which comes next; a person who follows next in order

SUFFERABLE – able to be tolerated

SUFFERANCE – tolerating, enduring patiently

SUFFRAGE – the right to vote

SUPERSEDE – to take the place or move into the position of

SUPPRESS – to stop or put to an end by force or authority

TENURE – the period or term for holding something such as an office

TERRITORY – a region controlled by or belonging to the government

THEREBY – by or through that

THEREFORE – for that reason

THEREIN – in that place

THEREOF – of that

TRAIN – a series or procession of things or acts

TRANQUILITY – calmness

TRANSIENT – not lasting, of short duration

TRIBUNALS – courts

TRY – examine according to law; to try in court

TYRANNY – cruel, oppressive, or unjust government

UNALIENABLE – not capable of being sold, separated, or taken. See *Inalienable.*

UNCONSTITUTIONAL – an act that violates the Constitution

UNDISTINGUISHED – indifferent; not discriminating; not selective; as in "whose known rule of warfare, is undistinguished destruction of all ages, sexes and conditions" (from the Declaration of Independence)

UNION – the group of independent states joined together

UNWARRANTABLE – unjustifiable

USURPATION – the wrongful taking of power or a right

VALIDITY – being legitimate and rigorous

VEST, VESTED – to place or to have placed in the control of a person or group

VETO – to reject or refuse to sign a bill from Congress

VIOLATION – disregarding an agreement or a right

VIZ. – abbreviation of the Latin word "videlicet" meaning "that is to say"

WANTING – lacking

WEIGHTS – ounces, pounds, tonnage, etc.

WELFARE – well-being, prosperity and happiness; national well-being promoted within restrictions permitted by the Constitution.

WHATSOEVER – of any kind

WORKS – actions, deeds, achievements

WRIT OF ELECTION – a writ ordering the holding of an election

WRIT – a formal legal document ordering some action

WRITS OF ELECTION – formal written documents ordering elections

YEA – a "yes" vote

ABOUT THE AUTHOR

Paul B. Skousen is an investigative journalist, writer, and teacher. He received his MA from Georgetown University in National Security Studies. He was a CIA military analyst and intelligence officer in the Situation Room at the Reagan White House. He has published several books on politics and history, and is a professor of communications and journalism.